THE
THREE
BOXES

Book of Kingdoms

ELAINE FAUCETT

WESTBOW
PRESS®
A DIVISION OF THOMAS NELSON
& ZONDERVAN

WestBow Press books may be ordered through booksellers or by contacting:

WestBow Press
A Division of Thomas Nelson & Zondervan
1663 Liberty Drive
Bloomington, IN 47403
www.westbowpress.com
844-714-3454

Scripture taken from the New King James Version® Copyright © 1982
by Thomas Nelson. Used by permission. All rights reserved.

ISBN: 978-1-6642-4922-6 (sc)
ISBN: 978-1-6642-4921-9 (e)

Print information available on the last page.

WestBow Press rev. date: 11/20/2021

This book is dedicated to my son, Willie Jojo Felder III, and my grandchildren, Milan Felder and Willie Bubba Felder IV.

But seek first the kingdom of God and His righteousness and all these things shall be added to you.
—Matthew 6:31

※ ☐ ⚞

NOTE TO THE READERS

This book is about kingdoms, specifically the kingdom of God. Although we live in the kingdom of the world, the kingdom of heaven is the destination for all citizens seeking eternal life with God. The New Testament begins in Matthew with John the Baptist announcing the kingdom. The scripture of Matthew 11:11(NKJV) says, "Assuredly I say to you, among those born of women but yet he who is least in the kingdom of heaven is greater than he." The kingdom of heaven belongs to those who have transferred from the kingdom of darkness (world kingdom) and now represent the kingdom of heaven right now, here on earth. They are greater than John because of the spiritual birth into the kingdom and now have an eternal life just like Adam before the fall.

The kingdom of God and the kingdom of heaven are the same but different. Perhaps, God's kingdom is his people, and heaven is the place where we live. For the redeemed are pilgrims traveling through the world kingdom and through Christ Jesus, who pierced the veil with His body. He has made us His sons and daughters, the children of God. Yet *The Three Boxes* was written for everyone, including the unchurched and maybe those asleep in the church. While reading *Book of Kingdoms*, keep in mind it comes from a vision and then through personal prayer and study of scripture. It is not a vision in the strict definition of the word, but it is a vision that simply inspires our imagination to see God's plan in a picture. The total revelation of the vision took six years.

Back in 2012, the original title was *The Three Boxes: The Book of Prosperity*. In my newborn spirit, I thought, *First seek God's kingdom, and get stuff from Him.* Honestly, I was not seeking God to get things. He had already done enough for me. My focus was on knowing Him, but at that time, I thought, *If He is pleased with me, He will bless me with gifts from the world kingdom*. After all, how else does God show His favor in this present life? With gladness and joy, I discovered His blessing in the revelation of *The Three Boxes: The Book of Kingdoms*. But lastly, while reading *Kingdoms*, stay prayerful, asking God for clear revelation through His Word as always.

With kindness,
Elaine Faucett

ACKNOWLEDGMENTS

Pastors Derry and Tammi Moten, thank you for your encouragement and support; it kept me in the last hours. May God bless the ministry and Abundant Life Worship Center.

Mary Faucett, thank you for all the hours you spent with me on this project; God used you again and again to fulfill His purpose. I could not have done it without you. I love you, Mom.

Katherine Parker, thank you for editing and reviewing the first draft of *Kingdoms*. We spent some amazing times processing this work, and I want to bless you for bringing this project to life.

To my friends Mr. and Mrs. Anderson, Cecilia, Nina, and Pastor Dennis Mukes of Faith Tabernacle MBC, thank you for your supporting prayers, godly advice, and keeping me going. You are true friends from the Lord.

To Dr. Frazer Thompson, PHD, PE, thank you and Spec Think Consulting, Situation Analysis for Creative Solutions, for your encouragement and efforts.

To Ms. Hattie Smith Miles, thank you for the opportunity to serve in the House of Acts. You are the best of the best. "To open their eyes, in order to turn them from darkness to light, and from the power of Satan to God, that they receive forgiveness of sins" (Acts 26:18).

To the true author, the Holy Spirit, who kept an unction on my spirit from revelation to the release of this book—He would not let me rest until it was done—thank You for allowing me the privilege to scribe this message.

THE VISION

I had never had a vision before; however, I did have a heavy encounter when my only son was shot, and I pleaded with God to save his life. God did. I wrote my testimony in my book *21 with a Bullet*, which I published in 2015. So, thankful for the modern-day miracle, I abandoned my secular life, no longer interested in all the posturing and perfect impressions that life had to offer. I was seeking a real relationship with the Highest God. My life changed. I would pray and study daily, never forgetting the miracle. I refused to be numbered among those who never came back to say, "Thank You," for the healing He had done.

I must say I know the difference between a dream and a vision. A dream is an unconscious state in which we experience events not in our present reality, but some people do daydream. A vision is something we experience in an awakened state.

Even before the popular movie *War Room*, I had a special place to pray and fellowship with the Father. It was two years after that fateful night that my life had been turned upside down. My life was not the pressed-down, shaken-together, and running-over type but just the *messy type*. After the shooting, I sold my house and was limited on space, so I used a room divider to section off the prayer space from the rest of the room.

One morning, I was praying in the spirit when I saw an image of a perfect square box presented before me. It was vividly detailed as if it were real. God would show me three different boxes in this vision.

The first box was wrapped like a present. It was bright red and covered with shining foil paper. It had a thick, garish gold bow on top. It looked like a loud Christmas present. Startled by its appearance, I gazed at the wonder. A gentle but firm voice said, "Open it." After removing the lid, I peered inside the brilliant red box. All kinds of things were inside it—things one would desire in this life, such as a house, a car, fine clothes, jewelry, and the abundance of things. I could best describe it as looking through a snow globe with a panoramic view.

Just as I was in awe of such a wondrous site, another box appeared. It was white. It was a plain cube with no bow or shining exterior, but oddly, it was attractive too. The gentle voice spoke again. "Look inside." Caught in some alternative dimension, I removed the white-lidded top and curiously peeped inside. It was *empty*. I kept looking for something to be there but saw nothing. As I moved closer to examine the inside, an illustrious bright light came beaming from the bottom of the empty box. Then a sweet-sounding voice called within the light, "Peace, love, joy, kindness, faith, hope." The room was filled with the familiar presence of God, His Holy Spirit.

Just as I was celebrating in His presence, a third box appeared.

This box was different from the other two, which was most intriguing because I did not understand it. The perfectly shaped box was wrapped in an exquisite golden fabric. It had no bow on top but was covered in twenty-four-carat woven gold with a craftsmanship that was royal in appearance. The instruction "Look inside" jolted me out of my daze. I looked inside to see a treasury of precious gems of different colors, cut and polished to perfection, causing a dance of lights, one upon the other. I was *bedazzled*.

Then I saw what appeared to be a large, white oval-shaped pearl intricately woven in gold. One of those priceless Fabergé eggs came to mind as I stared inside the royal jewelry box.

Stunned from the extraordinary vision, I finally said out loud, "What does this all mean?"

The Holy Spirit spoke clearly. "Seek the kingdom of God and His righteousness, and all these things will be given to you as well." Then it was over.

I sat there stunned, knowing it was unusual. I did not understand it.

It would take six years of revelation upon revelation to discover the true meaning of the three boxes.

They were kingdoms.

KINGDOM OF THE WORLD

The Material Kingdom

> For all that is in the world, the lust of the flesh and the lust of the
> eyes, and the pride of life is not of the Father but is of the world.
> —1 John 2:16

The first box was wrapped like a festive Christmas present. It represented the kingdom of the world, today's physical world. In the vision, the red box was shiny, exciting, and flamboyant. The voice invited me to look inside; it was filled with things we strive to achieve, possess, and experience. Satan's great hope is people will only seek the red box and never look outside it.

KINGDOM OF GOD

☐

Spiritual Kingdom

> Most assuredly, I say to you, unless one is born of water
> and Spirit, he cannot enter into the kingdom of God.
> —John 3:5

The second box in the vision was white and plain—nothing peculiar. Looking inside, I saw it was empty, and then an amazing light shone and filled the box. The white box had three significant signs. It was empty, it had brilliant light, and the voice sounded the "fruit of the Spirit." More important than the *presents* that filled the red box was *His presence*, which filled the second white box. His Holy Spirit undoubtedly overflowed into the entire atmosphere. The white box represented the spiritual kingdom of God.

KINGDOM OF HEAVEN

Eternal Kingdom

> And I, John saw the holy city, New Jerusalem coming down from God
> out of heaven from God, prepared as a bride adorned for her husband.
> —Revelation 21:2

The third box was most interesting, as the kingdom of God and the kingdom of heaven are the same but different in application. Through a detailed study of the kingdom, the Holy Spirit showed me the differences. The white box was clearly the presence of the Holy Spirit, but what did the third box with precious stones and a giant pearl in an intricately woven gold box represent?

As I was explaining the boxes to my pastors, Derry and Tammie Moten, they plainly told me, "You know the New Jerusalem comes down from heaven in a square gold box." The New Jerusalem is God's holy city and the eternal destination of those whose names are written in the Lamb's book of life. The gold box represents the eternal kingdom of heaven.

THE KINGDOMS

Kingdom of the World   Kingdom of God   Kingdom of Heaven

     □

Material   Spiritual   Eternal

The kingdoms of this World have become the Kingdoms of our
Lord and His Christ; and He will reign for ever and ever.
—Revelation 11:15

KINGDOM COMPARISONS

	Category	The Kingdom of the World	The Kingdom of God	The Kingdom of Heaven
1.	**Ruler**	Satan	Jesus	The Father
2.	**Character**	Harlot	Betrothed	Bride/Groom
3.	**Time**	Past	Present	Future
4.	**Spirit**	Babylon	Preparation	Wedding
5.	**Trinity**	Jesus	Holy Spirit	The Father
6.	**Gates**	Wide	Narrow	Pearl
7.	**Gifts**	Myrrh	Frankincense	Gold
8.	**Tripart-Man**	Body	Soul	Spirit
9.	**Evidence**	Works of the Flesh	Fruit of the Spirit	Faith
10.	**Ministry**	Condemnation	Reconciliation	Worship
11.	**Temple**	Outer Court	The Holy Place	Most Holy Place
12.	**Three Feasts**	Passover	Pentecost	Tabernacle
13.	**End Game**	Hell	Paradise	New Jerusalem

1. RULER

In the beginning, the kingdom of heaven, the kingdom of God, and the kingdom of the world were all one kingdom on earth. After humanity's fall, the kingdoms of heaven and God separated from the world, and the world gained a new ruler. The good news is God is the sovereign ruler over all things.

Kingdom of the World
Ruler: Satan

> "Now is the judgement of this world; now the ruler of this world will be cast out" (John 12:31).

God's kingdom and the kingdom of the world were one in Eden. God created man and gave him *rulership* over the earth. The earth was God's, but He put Adam in charge. Before that, Lucifer had been thrown out of heaven. Having lost his domain, he persuaded Adam to listen to him rather than to God. Upon Adam's disobedience to God's word, the covenant between God and man was broken. The curse of sin and death would now reign upon man and in the earth. Created with God's eternal spirit, man would now share the serpent's sin nature and die—first spiritually and then physically.

The new ruler was now Lucifer. However, with a change of position comes a new name. He was anointed Satan. Once God's highest angel, Lucifer was described as adorned with precious stones and perfect in beauty. His perfect beauty and wisdom created a pride that caused him to think he could rise above the throne of God. He was defeated and kicked out. He came to earth where he tricked Adam out of his inheritance. Now Jesus Christ, God's Son, would come to earth to return God's kingdom. In the process, Satan tried to entice Jesus. Satan said, "All this authority I will give You, and their glory; for this has been DELIVERED TO ME, and I will give it to whomever I wish" (Luke 4:6).

Satan is the new ruler of the world kingdom, where sin and death reign. This was not God's will for man, but Adam had broken the covenant, and the curses were sealed in the earth. Death remained king until Jesus came to earth, was sacrificed, and rose to life. The return to the Father's kingdom had begun, but now two distinct kingdoms would battle for our very souls.

ANCHOR POINT

The world kingdom is a temporary kingdom. Satan is still roaming around like a lion seeking whom he may devour. He is the prince of the air, keeping man occupied with the same conversation he gave Adam and Eve in the garden.

Kingdom of God
Ruler: Jesus Christ

> "You say rightly that I am a king. For this cause I have come into the world" (John 18:37).

Jesus was born a king and given gifts by the wise men. After He was taken into custody, Jesus said, "My kingdom is not of this world" (John 18:36). Christ's kingdom is a spiritual kingdom and is here now but also for the age to come. God sent Jesus down to return the kingdom back to man. Adam and Jesus were born without a sin nature. For that reason, Jesus is called the second Adam. But Jesus was both man and God, as He was raised from the dead. The Word of God became flesh and was clothed as the Messiah Jesus. He demonstrated His kingdom by healing diseases, casting out devils, and raising the dead. In the Father's future eternal kingdom of heaven, it's declared, "God will wipe away every tear from their eyes; there shall be no more death, nor sorrow, nor crying" (Revelation 21:4).

Before we pass from this world, we can only enter the kingdom of God through His Holy Spirit. Jesus told Nicodemus, "Unless one is born again, he cannot see the kingdom of God" (John 3:3). He was speaking of a spiritual rebirth. Jesus sacrificed His body to become the sin offering for the world, making it possible for us to become spiritually reborn and enter the kingdom of God. At the cross, Jesus said, "It is finished!" (John 19:30). He had fulfilled the law of sin and death, and restoration of the kingdom could begin.

The revelation of the three boxes was no one can enter the kingdom of heaven without first entering the kingdom of God. Jesus said, "But seek first the kingdom of God and His righteousness" (Matthew 6:33). Jesus is the way back to the Father's eternal kingdom, as "No one comes to the Father except through Me" (John 14:6). Jesus is Lord and ruler; He is the King of kings and Lord of all.

ANCHOR POINT

King Jesus's mission was to return the kingdom to His Father. He was sacrificed because of the chief priests' fear, and as they said, "Look, the world has gone after Him!" (John 12:19). But God's plan was to use their hatred to bring Christ to glory for the reconciliation of man, back to Himself.

Kingdom of Heaven
Ruler: The Father

> "The Lord has established His throne in heaven and His kingdom rules overall" (Psalm 103:19).

God the Father created the heavens and the earth through His Word. Then He created man to rule and tend the earth. He created man with His eternal spirit; man had a covenant with the Father, and there was no separation between them. He gave man all provisions in Eden's paradise on earth. But God wanted man to choose obedience, and in that obedience was the covenant between God and man. Man was told exactly what would happen if he chose not to believe Him. Whose word did Adam believe, the Father's or the serpent's? Today, we are faced with the same choice. "Choose for yourselves this day whom you will serve" (Joshua 24:15): the temporal world kingdom or the kingdom of God. The Father rules the kingdom of heaven because it is His authority to return His kingdom back to earth after the seventh trumpet of judgment. Just like in Eden, there will be no death, pain, or sorrow. "But only those who are written in the Lamb's Book of Life" (Revelation 21:27) will enter in the Father's permanent kingdom of heaven for eternal life.

ANCHOR POINT

The Father did not have to send His Son and make a new covenant; He did it out of His great love and mercy for us. He will make a new heaven and new earth (Revelation 21:1) to establish His kingdom once again on earth.

2. CHARACTER

The word *character* describes a distinctive personality; it is an illustration to understand the attributes and nature of a person or thing. Jesus's disciples asked, "Why do You speak to them in parables? He answered and said to them, Because It has been given to you to know the mysteries of the kingdom of heaven, but to them it has not been given" (Matthew 13:10). Those with eyes to see and ears to hear are permitted to understand.

Kingdom of the World
Character—Harlot

> "And on her forehead a name was written MYSTERY BABYLON THE GREAT, THE MOTHER OF HARLOTS AND ABOMINATIONS OF THE EARTH" (Revelation 17:5).

The world kingdom's character is like that of the harlot, the spiritual prostitute. The Jewish people, being regarded as the spouse of Yahweh, committed spiritual adultery with many participating in Baal worship (ritual sexual worship, sodomy, and religious prostitution) after accepting the covenant with God. The harlot is someone in intimate relationships without a covenant or, worse, in a covenant but unfaithful. The harlot's desire is to get more and more things out of the red box. The harlot is not interested in the spiritual things of the kingdom, as they are not useful for the world. "But the natural man does not receive the things of the Spirit of God, for they are foolishness to him, nor can he know them because they are spiritually discerned" (1 Corinthians 2:14). Spiritual harlots are self-reliant in relationship with God. They lead independent spiritual lives, following their own brand of spiritual doctrine outside the power of Christ. The harlot is mysticism, which the scripture refers to as "Mystery Babylon, the Great Mother Queen of Harlots" (Revelation 17:5). These *new age* spiritual religions are the old age Babylonian mystery religion, repackaged in a new shiny red box.

But God loves the world too. Rahab and Mary Magdalen were both prostitutes who became devoted followers of God. Because Jesus paid for our sins with His death, it is a free gift, and no works can purchase entrance into heaven. It cannot be earned; it is priceless. It does not matter whether you are a Rahab harlot or a Mary Magdalen. Each person must transfer from the world kingdom and be reborn into God's kingdom or else the sin nature remains.

When the spiritual harlot is reborn and filled with the Holy Spirit, she takes off the filthy rags and puts on the righteousness of Christ. In doing so, the harlot becomes the betrothed, beginning preparation for the wedding with the bridegroom, the Lamb of God, Jesus Christ.

All mankind becomes infirm and dies because Adam has passed down a sin nature to us. Blinded by the glamor of sin, the harlot can become reborn and receive the Holy Spirit. The harlot becomes the betrothed, and eternal life begins.

Kingdom of God
Character—Betrothed

> "For I am jealous for you with a godly jealously. For I have betrothed you to one husband, that I may present you as a chaste virgin to Christ" (2 Corinthians 11:2).

The character of person in the kingdom of God is the betrothed. The betrothed is someone waiting in promise of a marriage covenant. It means cutting off all intrusive relationships outside of the beloved and accepting Jesus Christ as our Lord and Savior. The process of letting go of the world and anything that would jeopardize the relationship with the beloved is omitted. In the world, the harlot can be flashy or fancy with a brash persona and usually wins over the quiet presence of the girl next door. But God's word says, "Do not let your adornment be merely outward—arranging the hair, wearing gold, or putting on fine apparel" (1 Peter 3:3). The mercy of the Lord allows us to come to Him as we are. If we are willing, He sanctifies us daily through His Holy Spirit. Everyone is born with the inherited sin nature from Adam. When the spiritual harlot becomes the betrothed, she or he becomes God's family. "Who were born, not of blood, nor of the will of the flesh, nor of the will of a man, but of God" (John 1:13).

Traditionally, when the betrothed becomes engaged, there is an exchange of gifts, showing the intention of commitment. Becoming members of God's eternal family, we receive the gift of the Holy Spirit, the deposit of His promise. During the engagement, the betrothed prepares for the upcoming celebration of the marriage. The betrothed has joined with Christ and represents His Body in the earth. The betrothed's robes get soiled from the world, but like laundry, we continually wash our robes in the blood of Jesus. Upon entering the kingdom of God, the betrothed stays faithful to Christ because He is looking for a bride without spot, wrinkle, or blemish.

ANCHOR POINT

The betrothed prepares for the upcoming marriage covenant. If we are faithful to the end, we will share in all that belongs to Christ, faithfully looking forward to the marriage feast with the beloved, Jesus Christ.

Kingdom of Heaven

Character—Bride

> "Come I will show you the bride, the Lamb's wife"
> (Revelation 21:9).

The kingdom of heaven is best described in character as the bride. The image of the New Jerusalem is the bride, the Lamb's wife. Jesus is the Lamb, who gave His life for our sins. The betrothed are God's people, the church, enjoined to Christ, who is the bridegroom, the Lamb of God. The wedding and consummation of the new covenant will take place in the New Jerusalem, and His children are all invited to the wedding feast. Jesus spoke in parables to illustrate the kingdom. The wedding feast best explains how God invited special people (His chosen nation), but they showed no interest, so He invited all nations. During the marriage feast, the King noticed someone not wearing the prescribed wedding clothes, and he evicted them out. Revelation 16:15 says, "Blessed is he who watches and keeps his garments." Entering the kingdom of God and receiving His Holy Spirit, we become clothed in His righteousness. The righteousness of Christ allows membership into God's holy family. In doing so, we become the body of Christ in the earth. The parable exemplifies someone who was invited, but instead of being covered in His righteousness, he or she was clothed in his or her own righteousness. All peoples are invited to the wedding, but endurance until the end is a requirement to receive the invitation to the Lamb's wedding feast. The New Jerusalem is the kingdom of heaven coming down from heaven to earth; it's described as a bride adorned for her husband.

A person's wedding day takes much time and preparation. He or she will be making a lifetime commitment and covenant with the betrothed. God is surely a covenant God. Understanding God's three main covenants in the Bible, you will understand God's will for man:

1. God's covenant with Adam
2. God's covenant with His nation of Israel
3. The new covenant through Jesus Christ—the bride and the bridegroom seal and consummate (make perfect) the new covenant in the New Jerusalem!

ANCHOR POINT

God's people are enjoined to Christ. Keeping the mindset of the betrothed, preparing for that most glorious day, the invitation to the wedding feast of the Lamb. The finalization of the new covenant, in the New Jerusalem, the bride of the Lamb. The children of God are the result of that holy marriage.

3. TIME

The three kingdoms are compared by the measure of time: past, present, and future. God is eternal, without beginning or ending. God's being is outside the realm of time. There never was a time that He did not exist. He created the world through His Word. He spoke it into existence. As He states, "I am Alpha and Omega, the beginning and the ending" (Revelation 1:8). He is yesterday, today, and forevermore.

Kingdom of the World
Time—Past

> "No one, having put his hand to the plow and looking back,
> is fit for the kingdom of God" (Luke 9:62).

For man, time was activated after the fall. Man would now have an *expiration date*—birth then death. Before the fall, man was created to live eternally. In God's kingdom, each day was glorious fellowship, and all provisions were given without toil. There was no past to regret, no deterioration, only heaven on earth. In life, much sadness comes from things like past decisions, the desire to recapture the past, missing a loved one, and remembering something we cannot attain. It brings us into reflection. The Beatles' popular song "Yesterday" was a tribute to the past and the sorrow of things lost. The past is something that is fixed; it cannot be changed. The popular Serenity Prayer "God grant me the wisdom to except the things I cannot change and the courage to change the things I can" is true wisdom.

Once the spirit leaves the body, the person continues to live on in spirit form, but the destination of the spirit is fixed at death. Therefore, Jesus pleads, "Repent for the kingdom of heaven is at hand" (Matthew 4:17). He does not want people to die in their sin; it is a final, fixed state.

The world kingdom and Satan, who is the ruler of this world, have a fixed *past*, a short present, and a condemned *future*. He cannot change that. The scripture tells us, "Woe to the inhabitants of earth and the sea! For the devil has come down to you, having great wrath, because he knows that he has a short time" (Revelation 12:12). Satan has little time to rule, and he knows the truth: the world is already judged. He is like a man on death row. He is still alive but condemned to die. Satan's mission is to take people with him. He is furious because God has given man a return to his first estate. Satan cannot get a do-over. He is like the jealous woman who lost her man and wants revenge. The past deals with looking back in regret, desire, yearning, and lusting over this life.

ANCHOR POINT

The past is a rearview mirror, smaller than the windshield. Looking behind too long can cause a wreck. Stay out of the rearview and live forward in Christ.

Kingdom of God
Time—Present

> "Therefore, if anyone is in Christ, he is a new creation: old things have passed away, behold all things have become new" (2 Corinthians 5:17).

The present time is associated with the kingdom of God because of His presence. At first sight, the white box was empty. I looked intently, as the first box, the red one, was filled with lavish worldly presents, while the second one was filled with His holy presence. In the present time, we still have choices. Some present choices may be impacted by past actions, but the present choice that matters is choosing the Lord as our Savior today. The *time is now* to enter the kingdom of God. We never know the day or time we will be called from here. If you wait and die in your sin, your future will be fixed in judgment. The past may be fixed, but in the present, there is still a choice. Every man has the choice as to whom he will serve. Satan wants us to keep waiting, not trusting, and hopes time will run out and our judgment will be final, just like his.

Although there were no tangible gifts in the white box, it signals to seek the spiritual kingdom of God and receive the gift of eternal life from the Holy Spirit. The white box is empty because you cannot see Spirit. Most people do not want the plain white box because there is nothing of value they can see. Rather, they choose the red gift box with the glamor of the world. Jesus tells us to seek the imperishable things of heaven, for the kingdom of God is not tangible. You may miss it if you're looking for some kind of "religious experience." It's only discernable to those who have been reborn in the Holy Spirit through Jesus Christ. "For the message of the cross is foolishness to those who are perishing, but to us who are being saved it is the power of God" (1 Corinthians 1:18). Remember the Holy Spirit is a gentleman; He will never force His presence upon you. You must choose Him. Only in the present moment can you experience His Presence. Once you start drifting to the past, unless you are repenting, you lose His Presence because the past belongs to the world. He will *present* you faultless before the presence of His glory if you choose Him and endure until the end.

ANCHOR POINT

Only in the present can you experience the presence of His Spirit. It is the gift of God. Staying in the present requires trust and faith, and it is impossible to please Him without it.

Kingdom of Heaven
Time—Future

> "For I know the thoughts that I think toward you, says the Lord, thoughts of peace and not of evil, to give you a hope and a future" (Jeremiah 29:11).

In my vision, the gold box had a large white pearl surrounded by multicolored precious gems. The box was wrapped in a royal golden fabric in contrast to the brash red box. The kingdom of heaven is the future home of those whose names are written in the Lamb's book of life. The book of Revelation speaks to the outcome of man's future with God. "I will show you things which must take place after this" (Revelation 4:1). When Jesus's disciples asked Him, "How should we pray?" He gave us the model prayer: "Thy kingdom come, thy will be done, on earth, as it is in heaven" (Matthew 6:9–13). Jesus tells us what God's will is; it's His future kingdom to come! He needs us to enter His spiritual kingdom of God while on earth.

The "on earth as it is in heaven" (Matthew 6:10) is now within us as evidenced by the Holy Spirit teamed with the Lord's future Holy City, the New Jerusalem. "Now I saw a new heaven and a new earth, for the first heaven and the first earth had passed away" (Revelation 21:1). The condition of this fallen world disqualifies the kingdom of heaven on earth as it is now. The kingdom of heaven is the kingdom of the age to come. It is the future and destination promised to the saints.

The past is fixed, the present is a choice, but the future is determined upon the choices we make in the present. God will give us our full rights as His people when we come into the kingdom of heaven—to enter His gates and never perish. On that day, thorns, thistles, and the things that came into the world will disappear; then there will be glorious freedom from sin. Let this future hope strengthen you while you are living in this deeply fallen world.

ANCHOR POINT

Trusting in His Word, we can clearly see our futures. If you can't determine yours, ask Him to show you, His kingdom.

4. SPIRIT

The spirit comparisons are illustrated by the dominant atmospheres of each kingdom. Each spirit is particular and carries a distinct purpose. The Spirit is the leader and ushers in each kingdom's *End Game*.

Kingdom of the World
Spirit—Babylon

> "Come out of her my people, lest you share in her sins, lest
> you receive of her plagues" (Revelation 18:4).

The Spirit of Babylon is a place of spiritual power in opposition to God. Babylon was the first world kingdom on earth. Nimrod was the ruler. Genesis 10:10 says, "And the beginning of his kingdom was Babel, Erech, Accad and Calneh in the land of Shinar." The secular world lists the Accadian (Akkad) kingdom as the first empire in Mesopotamia and the Sumerian people as the first known civilization. The word *Babylon* means confusion and mixture and is associated with different names—Babel, Cradle of Civilization, Mesopotamia, Land of Shinar, Sumer, Sumerian, Chaldean, Baghdad, Assyria, and Samaria, well as present-day Iraq. Nimrod is most noted for building the tower of Babel, symbolic for rebellion against God's command. God told the people to spread out and fill the earth, but Nimrod entreated the people, saying, "Let us make a name" (Revelation 10:4). Nimrod encouraged them to become spiritually independent from God. But man is created to worship something higher than himself, so Nimrod instituted himself as a proxy god, and Baal worship began its course after the flood. Babylon was the first global government to include one political and religious system. The spirit of Babylon birthed pagan and occult worship, which is in essence self-worship.

Mystery religions were established first in Babylon, and from there, pagan worship spread to various cultures around the world. Egyptian, Greek, and Roman cultures are rooted in Babylon. God has called His people to come out of the Babylonian world system and to seek His eternal kingdom through Jesus Christ and His Holy Spirit.

ANCHOR POINT

The spirit of Babylon is inside the red box—all the heart's desires mixed with the entanglements of pursuing them. It is best described as a life outside of Christ, while embracing all ambition in the world.

Kingdom of God
Spirit—Preparation

> "Then the kingdom of heaven shall be likened to ten virgins who took their lamps and went out to meet the bridegroom. Now 5 of them were wise and 5 of them were foolish" (Matthew 25:1–2).

The spirit of preparation is the endeavor for heaven's glory. The preparation is designed to sanctify us. It is preparation for eternal kingdom living. This is done by leading a daily lifestyle of repentance, prayer, and humility. The newly born into the kingdom are babes in the Lord, not knowing much about the new life. The church is for fellowship and for preparation, edification, learning, and increasing spiritual aptitude while living in the world. Always remember everyone in the church used to be in the world and has different levels of maturity, and everyone gets called out of the world differently.

Fellowship safely prepares us to exercise discernment through interaction with other church members, as "Iron sharpens Iron" (Proverbs 27:17). Jesus compared the kingdom of God to a mustard seed, as preparation leads to the growth of the tiny mustard seed into a large great tree. Accepting the Lord means to seek Him daily. It is not a one-time experience, where you *get saved* and wear white on the first Sunday because *you are in*. The parable of the wise and foolish virgins demonstrates the end reward for kingdom preparation. The ten virgins were invited to the wedding feast but had to wait for the bridegroom. Although all maids were initially prepared—or *saved*—only half kept their lamps trimmed. Upon the call of the bridegroom, the unprepared had to go to the market for oil. On their return, they found the door locked. Only those prepared with oil, made it in the door.

ANCHOR POINT

The kingdom of God is spiritual, and preparation is a continuum; through faith and the deposit of the Holy Spirit, we prepare to become like the wise ones, who made it in the door.

Kingdom of Heaven
Spirit—Wedding

> "For the marriage of the Lamb has come, and His wife has made herself ready" (Revelation 19:7).

The wedding is the ultimate spirit of celebration. That spirit is encompassed in the royal wedding. Millions of people watched the fairytale wedding of Prince Harry and Duchess Meghan. It had the atmosphere of the royal wedding spirit. It was the Cinderella story of a biracial commoner who married the prince of England. The media followed every detail concerning the upcoming royal nuptials. When the day arrived, as Meghan came down the aisle at George's Chapel, the whole world paused to see her entrance. Surprisingly, she chose a plain white wedding sheath, absent embellishment. The only sparkle was in her eyes and the diamond Queen Mary tiara she borrowed from the royal family's collection.

At first glance, I was disappointed in the gown, expecting an elaborate design to match the once-in-a-lifetime royal occasion. But as the wedding unfolded, the glory of the elitist procession made the classic white gown noble and befitting of the new princess that she was. Meghan's dress was fabulously perfect. The simple, elegant white dress made allowance for the ultra-royal occasion. The more I watched, the more I applauded the dress. Just like the world, I was expecting the Princess Di glamor in the royal gown that Princess Meghan would don. But she chose a simple classic dress because of the magnitude of the royalty she was signing into.

In my vision, the kingdom of God is represented by the plain white box. The metaphor for Meghan's dress choice as she married into the wealthy royals is represented by the rich gold box with precious stones and a giant pearl. The church is enjoined to Christ in preparation for the royal wedding of the Lamb. His people are those *who endure* to have their names written in the Lamb's book of life. The spirit of the wedding tells us, "Blessed are those who are called to the marriage supper Feast of the Lamb!" (Revelation 9:9). This is an invitation-only event.

ANCHOR POINT

The wedding spirit is the ultimate celebration. God uses it as the example to describe the new covenant promise between God and man. All things will be made new.

5. TRINITY

The one and only God exists as three distinct persons: God the Father, God the Son, and God the Holy Spirit. This is the mystery of God. He is not a created being; He is the Creator and Ruler of all heaven and earth. "For there are three that bear witness in heaven, the Father, the Word and the Holy Spirit; and these three are one" (1 John 5:7).

The Kingdom of the World
The Trinity—Jesus

> "And the Word became flesh and dwelt among us, and we beheld His glory" (John 1:14).

If Adam never sinned, there would be no need for Jesus to come to earth as a man. He became the Passover Lamb of God, qualifying Him to take the scroll and break the seals, which are all the curses. God could have kept us in our current sinful state, but His mercy and grace compelled Him to send His Son. "For God so loved the world that He gave His only begotten Son, that whoever believes in Him should not perish but have everlasting life" (John 3:16). Jesus came to heal what happened in Eden. Adam fell by believing the serpent over God's Word. "For the wages of sin is death" (Romans 6:23). On Calvary, when Christ died, the temple curtain tore, symbolizing the end of separation between God and man. Man could now have access to God again. Inside every father is the seed of his offspring. Words come from the inside to the outside, as Jesus said, "I am in My Father" (John 14:20). "In the beginning was the Word and the Word was with God, and the Word was God" (John 1:1). That Word was made flesh, and His name is Jesus.

Adam was created with God's eternal spirit but lost the heavenly kingdom on earth. Jesus is called the second Adam because He was victorious over death and offers us a do-over. Only those who believe and endure will have what Adam lost in the first place. The issue is that most people do not see the need for a Savior. They say being a decent person is sufficient. Not understanding their inherently sinful nature, many believe their own righteousness is a moral compass for salvation. We as a nation have become so spiritually independent and so impressed with ourselves. Some even question as to why Jesus had to die at all for them, seeing no darkness in themselves. Luke 11:35 says, "Therefore take heed that the light which is in you is not darkness." Gnosticism speaks of a thousand points of light. If you do not know, google it. Some say they have no need for a Savior because they already have the light. They misunderstand the fact that we are born in God's image and at times reflect that image. But we also reflect the sinful nature that separates us from God. Jesus's sacrifice allows us to receive God's Holy Spirit and enter into the kingdom, as He is the Father of lights. It keeps us plugged into the right power source, giving us the understanding of why Jesus is called the "True Light" (John 1:9).

ANCHOR POINT

The temporal light of the world can be mistaken for the true light of Christ. Jesus is the true light, as He is "The light of the world" (John 8:12). Always check your power source.

Kingdom of God
Trinity—Holy Spirit

> "And there are three that bear witness in earth, the Spirit,
> the water and the blood" (1 John 5:8).

The white box was empty, and so was the tomb! But as I kept looking, it was filled with a bright white light. The kingdom of God is on earth now; it is spiritual, ushered in by the Holy Spirit on Pentecost. The Holy Spirit is the Spirit of the triune God. Those who have been reborn receive it and are God's people, His church. The church is not a building; it's a meeting place to worship and fellowship together, a place of fortification as the kingdom of light is fighting for the souls living in the kingdom of darkness, while the kingdom of darkness is fighting for the souls of those in the kingdom of light. The Holy Spirit is the helper, the advocate, the promise from the Father. He told the disciples it's best that He goes away. "For if I do not go away, the Comforter will not come unto you" (John 16:7). He is the same Holy Spirit He gave Adam, but after sin, Adam's eternal spirit fused with sin, resulting in death. Adam's DNA changed from light to dark, from life to death. His body would now age and die because his spirit was tainted with no godly power to preserve it. For example, a piece of fruit is healthy, but after time, it perishes and becomes rotten. A similar concept exists in life: our bodies perish in time. But it was not so in the beginning.

Before the fall, Adam and Eve only knew God's voice. The serpent spoke with Eve, verifying that she knew the difference between what God said and what he was telling her. After disobedience, they immediately felt a strange spirit, a spirit of *fear, inadequacy, vulnerability, and feeling ashamed*. They felt they were not good enough. God said, "Who told you that you were naked?" (Genesis 3:11). God had never told them those things. Those feelings came from a different spirit. From then on, man would have to discern between the voice of the Holy Spirit and the soft mimicking voice of the garden serpent.

ANCHOR POINT

The Holy Spirit is the Helper; it is the very Spirit of God. Without the Holy Spirit, religion and traditions dominate in the earth. You must receive the Holy Spirit to enter the kingdom of God and ultimately the kingdom of heaven.

Kingdom of Heaven
Trinity—Father

> "But as many as received Him, to them He gave the right to
> become children of God, to those who believe in His name;
> who were born not of blood, nor of the will of flesh, nor of
> the will of man but of God" (John 1:12–13).

Adam and Eve listened to the serpent and then hid themselves from God. Suddenly they felt something they had never felt before, *fear*. This was new, because prior to sin, they had felt secure and complete. Someone had to tell them this. This new feeling came with the spirit from the tree of knowledge. They were now under the influence. The glory that covered them was gone; the people they used to be were no longer. They had lost their covenant. They sewed together fig leaves to camouflage the fear and embarrassment that separated them from their creator, God the Father. The kingdom on earth was now dark and light. These two kingdoms would now war with each other and have two different fathers. The fathers come from two dynamically opposed kingdoms that vie for the souls of men. The Father of Light seeks to bring people out of darkness. The father of darkness seeks the children of light to bring them back into darkness.

When Jesus told some Jews about the Father, they responded that their father was Abraham. They lacked understanding about the spiritual kingdom that is the foundation of all life. Jesus plainly told them, "Because you are not able to listen to My word, you are of your father the devil and the desires of your father you want to do" (John 8:42–44).

When Adam listened to the serpent, spiritually, he became a child of the devil. The politically correct term is *a child of the world*. Satan is not what people think he is. He is charming, hilarious, and full of worldly wisdom and appears as a beautiful creation, but conceals his true identity. He is the father of lies. Satan is known for music and entertainment and is skilled in distraction so people will continue with him. But God the Father is concerned with reconciliation for eternal life. He has arranged salvation through His Son. As Jesus said, "I am the way, the truth and the life. No one comes to the Father except through Me" (John 14:6).

ANCHOR POINT

The Father, Son, and Holy Spirit are all God, separate yet one. The Father sent His Son and then His Holy Spirit to redeem us. It is the mystery of God.

6. GATES

A gate is an entry point to protect the inhabitants and keep out the unwelcome. Gates are outside the perimeter of a dwelling place, home, or city. Kingdom gates are described by the conditions required to pass into each one.

Kingdom of the World
Gates—Wide

> "For wide is the gate and broad is the way that leads to destruction, and there are many who go in by it" (Matthew 7:13).

Matthew 22 talks about the wedding feast parable. The first guests invited were not interested. The king told them to go into the main highways and invite as many as they could. The day of the feast someone was found not wearing the prescribed wedding robes and was thrown outside the gates. The violation was this; they provided their own covering. The kingdom of the world is the wide gate, the main highway. The world gate is wide enough for the masses to get through. It allows for all universal, self-created pathways that are all-inclusive. The people on this road are confident and proud they have chosen such a brazen path. All mankind is born into the world of the wide gate.

Jesus tells us how hard it is for a rich man to enter the kingdom of heaven. His reliance on wealth provides a false security in the solutions to life's maladies. He may think his wealth is an impregnable defense, a high wall of safety. When entering through the narrow gate, he would try to bring his entire kingdom into the kingdom of God. But the narrow gate cannot accommodate it. The rich man has worldly power. He can purchase his way out of tribulations that would otherwise humble a person to the Lord. David said, "Let their table become a snare and a trap, a stumbling block and a recompense to them" (Romans 11:9).

The wide gate is a pleasant find; it is easy to navigate. It allows for a limitless amount of luggage on the journey. The world kingdom is Broadway, and the whole world is going in that direction. When a fork in the road comes, a decision is at stake. Jesus said, "You cannot dine at both tables, mixing the kingdoms together." Many churches are promoting coexisting religions, sharing the vision that we are all just taking a different route, but all paths lead to God. The wide path encourages us to embrace all lifestyles. But Jesus teaches obedience, to love the sinner but hate the sin. The god of this world has blinded many to think they can stay on Broadstreet and still enter in. "Wide is the gate, and broad is the road that leads to destruction"

(Matthew 7:13). But they end up with eternal separation from God. Eternal separation would be like living with people in an eternal prison and no protection from the infliction of pain. There is no goodness, only darkness, and God is not there.

ANCHOR POINT

The wide gate is universal and the road most traveled. Too easily distracted by what is popular and pleasurable, those who go through the wide gate follow man instead of God.

The Kingdom of God
Gates—Narrow

> "Because narrow is the gate and difficult is the way which leads to life, and there are few who find it" (Matthew 7:14).

Like the kingdom of God, the white box appears as if nothing is inside because it is a spiritual kingdom. But if we continue to seek His presence, He will find us and answer. Jesus said only a few find it. Be arduous because the Spirit is like the wind. It is narrow because there is only one way to eternal life. It demands full repentance, denial of self, self-examination, and submission to Jesus as our Lord and Savior. Any time we become slack in seeking His presence, the road will widen a little at a time, until the way disappears. The kingdom of God is like the plain box, nothing appealing from the outside. But after we meet Jesus, the process of eliminating useless baggage begins.

Some are deceived, thinking they can add God to their already-made kingdom and enter in. No, it is only you and God. Your personal kingdom will not fit through the narrow gate. It must be left behind. The rich man asked Jesus what he must do to get eternal life. The rich man said, "I have kept all the commandments." Jesus told to him to sell all his belongings and give to the poor, and then he would have treasure in heaven. The rich man was not willing, so he went away in sadness. He loved the flashy red box more than the plain, empty white box. To enter, we are not required to sell our possessions, but anything that stands above the Lord needs to be released.

People ask, "What do you think about worldly lifestyles?" My response is "I have no opinion. Whatever people do is their choice. I follow God's Word for my life as a citizen of the kingdom of heaven. The world kingdom is the world kingdom, and we follow whoever is our king."

One issue in today's Christian church is the similarity to the world. You might see pastors preaching about prosperity as the blessing, with elders dressing lavishly and flamboyantly. They are selling the benefits like a commodity, rather than teaching sanctification to truly enter the presence of His Holiness. Not all who sound religious are godly people. Just because someone professes the Lord does not mean he or she will enter the kingdom of heaven.

The Kingdom of God
Gates—Narrow

Christians attaching miracles, wealth, and even healing as signs and wonders may miss the entrance to the narrow gate. The narrow way is a difficult one that will take us through hardships and difficult seasons. The narrow gate is away from the crowd and does not come with bells and whistles. But He gives us strength to endure. Jesus tells us to cheer up for He has overcome the world. Instructions are as follows:

1.   Seek the narrow gate.
2.   Walk through it.
3.   Stay on it until the end.

Luke 13:24 says, "Make every effort to enter through the narrow door."

ANCHOR POINT

Jesus gave His life for the opportunity to choose salvation. If you seek and find Him in the secret place, then you may find the narrow gate.

The Kingdom of Heaven
Gates—Pearl

> "And the twelve gates were twelve pearls, each individual gate was of one pearl" (Revelation 21:21).

The third box in the vision represents the kingdom of heaven. It looked like woven twenty-four-carat golden fabric. But in the inside were countless precious stones and a giant pearl. The kingdom of heaven is an actual place. Revelation illustrates the Holy City, the New Jerusalem. Before my salvation, when I heard the old song "When the Saints Come Marching In," the only thing I could imagine was the New Orleans Saints running into the Superdome.

The pearly gates are the entrance to Zion, the New Jerusalem. Only those whose names have been written in the Lamb's book are permitted, as nothing impure or harmful will ever enter. Although we are all born sinners, only those washed in the blood of Jesus will become enjoined to Christ. The betrothed will be invited to the wedding feast of the Lamb. Psalm 24:7 says, "Lift up your heads, O you gates! And be lifted up, you everlasting doors! And the King of Glory shall come in." He says, "Open the gates so a righteous nation can come in." The righteous nation are those in that number, those who have accepted Christ and have washed their robes in the blood of the Lamb. Too many people think they can just add God on Sunday and be reconciled with Him—no change in the spirit but giving gestures of service covering the carnality of daily living. No one can work their way into the kingdom. Salvation is a gift that Jesus already paid for. The hope is that our name is in that number to enter heaven's pearly gates for all eternity.

ANCHOR POINT

Brides wear pearls for honor and loyalty. The pearl gates are a picture of the purity and durability of the kingdom. They will last forever, just like the kingdom of heaven.

7. GIFTS

The three wise men brought gifts to the Messiah. "They presented gifts to Him: gold, frankincense and myrrh" (Matthew 2:11). Each gift in the scripture—gold, frankincense, and myrrh—is placed in the same order as the kingdom boxes, but it starts with gold, ultimately representing the kingdom of heaven, the highest kingdom. It is the place where the Father lives.

Kingdom of the World
Gifts—Myrrh

> "Then they gave Him wine mingled with myrrh to drink
> but He did not take it" (Mark 15:23).

The red box / world kingdom contains all the world's woes because of the bitterness of sin and death. The Semitic meaning of the word *myrrh* is "bitter," and it is classified as a sour herb. Jesus came into the world kingdom because Adam had sinned, and death had entered the entire human race. Jesus *willingly* gave Himself as a living sacrifice to redeem us back to the Father. He is a living sacrifice because He offered His life while He was still alive. The myrrh was given at His birth, signifying the thorns in the crown, the cup on the cross, and then the spice used for His burial.

When the time came to fulfill the scripture, Jesus went to the garden and prayed a sorrowful prayer of bitterness. He said, "O My Father, If it is possible, let this cup pass from Me, nevertheless, not as I will, but as You will" (Matthew 26:39). As the Son of Man and the second Adam, Jesus anguished over what He was about to face. He then sweat tears of blood but was obedient to His Father's will. Then He was arrested.

After He had been humiliated and scourged, they mocked Him with a thorny crown, which they pushed into His head. The scripture is silent on the plant used, but the myrrh plant has long spikes. After they nailed Him, they offered Him wine mixed with myrrh to dull the pain of His crucifixion. Jesus refused to dilute His sacrifice. The gift of myrrh represents the bitterness of suffering and death. Jesus willingly drank this bitter cup to give us the gift of salvation, eternal life.

ANCHOR POINT

The gift of myrrh represents Christ's agony for the bitterness of sin and death. Jesus said, "Shall I not drink the cup which My Father has given me?" (John 18:11).

The Kingdom of God
Gifts—Frankincense

> "You are a priest forever, according to the order of Melchizedek" (Hebrews 7:17).

Jesus was given frankincense at His birth. The frankincense depicts the priesthood. Jesus brought the new covenant so all mankind could reconcile with God. With the new covenant comes a change of law and the priesthood. The Levites were the old covenant priesthood. The job of the high priest was to petition God for the sins of the people, but the Levitical high priest was replaced once he died. Only the Levitical priests were allowed behind the curtain in the Holy Place. They were required to burn the special blend of frankincense in the temple. At Jesus's death, the temple curtain tore, signifying the end of separation.

First Peter 2:9 says, "You are a chosen generation, a royal priesthood, a holy nation, His own special people." The frankincense represents Jesus as our High Priest in the order of Melchizedek, an eternal priesthood for the eternal kingdom He has prepared for us. Frankincense also represents the intercessory prayers of the saints. "Each one holding a harp and golden bowls full of incense, which are the prayers of the saints" (Revelation 5:8). God needs His people to help minister to the world. Jesus states, "The harvest is truly plentiful, but the laborers are few" (Matthew 9:37).

ANCHOR POINT

The gift of frankincense signifies the priesthood and prayers of His people from earth to heaven. The duty of the priests is intercession for people and ministering to the lost. The people in the kingdom of God are His royal priesthood.

Kingdom of Heaven
Gifts—Gold

> "And on the cloud sat One like the Son of Man, having on
> His head a golden crown, and in His hand a sharp sickle"
> (Revelation 14:14).

Jesus was given gold at His birth. The gift of gold represents His royal kingdom. In my vision, the third box was an intricate gold cube with precious jewels. There are 361 passages mentioning gold in the Bible because gold is significant to God's eternal kingdom. The gold the wise men presented is mentioned first, as there is no kingdom higher than the kingdom of heaven. The gold signifies Jesus's status as the king of glory, His royalty in the kingdom. In John's revelation, there are golden crowns, golden sashes, golden candlesticks, golden censors, golden vials, golden trumpets, golden bowls, a golden altar, golden streets, and a golden measuring stick to measure the golden city of the New Jerusalem. Although Jesus was given gold at his birth, there is no mention of Jesus ever possessing gold in His earthly lifetime. However, rich citizens were enamored by Him as he kept company with those who seemed to have little value in the eyes of the world. When people said they wanted to follow Him, He told them, "But the Son of Man has nowhere to lay His head" (Matthew 8:20). If you want to follow Christ, this is not His home. He made it plain that His kingdom was not of this world, so if your sole desire is for worldly riches, you have the wrong kingdom. But the kingdom of heaven is full of gold. In heaven, Jesus is described as dressed in royal garments with a golden crown and sash and ruling on a golden throne. Solomon's temple was a shadow and copy of the heavenly kingdom. It was built to house the Ark of the Covenant, the very presence of God, which was covered with pure gold and precious gems. God gave specific design instructions to Moses for His holy nation. But Israel, God's chosen nation, was unfaithful. The gold was stripped, the temple was destroyed, and they were sent to exile in Babylon. Jesus came to restore His eternal kingdom of heaven back to man with the golden New Jerusalem.

The gift of gold given to Jesus at birth represents His eternal kingdom of the New Jerusalem, which comes down from heaven in a square gold box. It is the residence of all heavenly citizens of the kingdom of God.

8. TRIPART MAN

God created man's body from the dust of the earth. He breathed the breath of life into his nostrils, and man became a living soul. Man is composed of three parts: body, soul, and Spirit. Each composition is discussed in relation to the kingdom of the world, kingdom of God, and kingdom of heaven.

Kingdom of the World
Tripart Man—Body

> "All flesh is as grass, and all the glory of man as the flower of the grass. The grass withers and its flower falls away, but the Word of the Lord endures forever" (1 Peter 1:24).

Man's body is made from the dust of the earth. The mass of the human body is 99 percent oxygen, carbon, hydrogen, nitrogen, calcium, and phosphorus, the minerals in the earth. That is a scientific fact. The physical body is the material part of man. Both the body and the world kingdom are physical, temporal, and perish over time. Satan's kingdom is designed is to keep people fixed on the flesh and living on bread alone. The elites feel their physical DNA is superior to the normal person's. Many have occult mystery knowledge that has been passed down from generation to generation and comes from Eden's tree of knowledge. This ancient occult knowledge has ruled and built the world kingdom through science and evolution. In Satan's kingdom, man evolves and becomes a god. The result is the illumination of man. This is called apotheosis. The apotheosis of George Washington is an example of the elites' true beliefs about their status. A painted fresco on the dome of the US Capitol shows Washington ascending and becoming a god. This is what the serpent promised Eve in the garden, only for her to find out differently later. After Adam sinned, God told him, "From dust you are, And to dust you shall return" (Genesis 3:19). But a person saved should live as in 2 Corinthians 4:7: "But we have this treasure in earthen vessels, that the excellence of the power may be of God and not of us."

ANCHOR POINT

The sanctified body is in covenant with the Lord, becoming a temple filled with His Holy Spirit, a vessel of honor to be used by God. Look forward to the transformation of a gloried body, one that never dies or gets old or sick. That is His promise.

Kingdom of God

Tripart Man—Soul

> "For the Word of God is living and powerful and sharper than any two-edged sword, piercing even to the division of soul and spirit" (Hebrews 4:12).

The soul is composed of the will, emotions, intellect (mind), and heart; it makes up the personality. It is our choices. The soul belongs to the spiritual kingdom of God because we must make a spiritual choice to enter. The analogy of a car demonstrates the dynamics between the body, soul, and spirit. The body of a car is like the human body. Ford and Mercedes Benz are cars but have different exteriors. The engine is like the spirit; when missing, it is dead. The soul is the steering wheel of the body, it turns to the desire of the driver. When God made man, He breathed into his nostrils, and man became a living soul. He wanted man to choose (using his soul) to obey Him. When Adam chose to believe the serpent, man inherited the same consequence as the serpent. Sin and death became fused with the eternal spirit in man. Adam now inhabited a new kind of spirit, infused with death and passed down to every man thereafter.

The Word of God is so powerful that it pierces the soul. The word of God does spiritual surgery and divides the soul from the spirit. The spirit is loosened from the sinful nature and set free. "Therefore if the Son makes you free, you shall be free indeed!" (John 8:36).

Eternal life then begins as the spirit has been freed from death. "Who were born, not of blood, nor of the will of the flesh, nor of the will of man, but of God" (John 1:13).

However, warfare for the soul continues as spirit and flesh battle throughout life. The mind needs to be renewed everyday as it is in the process of evolving towards God. But the Spirit is set free. As the Word says in 3 John 1:2, "Beloved, I pray that you may prosper in all things and be in health, just as your soul prospers."

ANCHOR POINT

The soul is our choice center. We are born with a sinful nature and with the soul and spirit fused together. We can choose to seek God and receive His Holy Spirit, and His Word will divide, setting the soul free. Thus, we become reborn as a new creation in Christ Jesus, and eternal life begins.

Kingdom of Heaven
Tripart Man—Spirit

> "Nevertheless do not rejoice in this, that the spirits are subject to you, but rather rejoice because your names are written in heaven" (Luke 10:20).

The tripart man is body, soul, and spirit. Our body perishes because of Adam's transgression, but God gives us a soul to choose salvation through Jesus's death. We receive His Holy Spirit and transfer from the kingdom of darkness into the kingdom of light.

Jesus's sole mission was to become a sacrifice and fulfill the law to establish the kingdom of heaven on earth. At the cross, He said, "It is finished" (John 19:30). Those who accept Christ are now citizens of the kingdom of heaven. Jesus did not come to save flesh; He came to save our soul, which determines where our spirit will live eternally, either in heaven or hell. Sometimes people think if someone's flesh does not get healed, it indicates that God is not with them. Jesus is concerned with our salvation so we can live in His permanent kingdom without suffering, eternally. His desire is for us to escape from the world kingdom and transfer into His kingdom of light. The spirit will live with God or be eternally separated from Him. To be eternally separated is probably like living in a perpetual horror movie.

The Word tells us we groan in this body, and when the tent is taken down, we are given a heavenly body, fit for the kingdom of heaven. The spirit encourages us not to give up, although the outer body is perishing as our inner spirit is renewed day by day. It is the spirit that is eternal because it is from the breath of God. The soul determines where our spirit will spend all eternity, for it is God's good pleasure to return His kingdom, but we must choose while living in the world kingdom, before our flesh expires.

ANCHOR POINT

God does not change; He will not change. We have a choice to be with Him eternally or to be eternally separated. The spirit in us is *eternal*.

9. EVIDENCE

Evidence is an outward sign that furnishes proof of something. Each kingdom has certain indicators that shape its validity. The works of the flesh, the fruit of the Spirit, and faith are hallmark characteristics for each kingdom.

Kingdom of the World
Evidence—Works of the Flesh

> "Now the works of the flesh are evident, which are adultery, fornication, uncleanness, lewdness, idolatry, sorcery, hatred, contentions, jealousies, outbursts of wrath, selfish ambitions, dissensions, heresies, envy, murders, drunkenness, revelries … those who practice such things will not inherit the kingdom of God" (Galatians 5:19–21).

The kingdom of the world is ruled by the flesh, driven by the power to obtain all the heart's desires. In a moment of time, desires of the material world appeared in the red box. Scripture notes that the lust of the eye, the lust of the flesh, and the pride of life are not from God but from the world. Lust is the desire to possess or have things that have visual appeal. These become manifested as evidence when material and world power become life's focus. Works of the flesh can be big, small, internal, or external. The internal ones are anger, slander, deceit, greed, envy, hatred, and selfish ambition, and external acts include murder, sexual immorality, witchcraft, idolatry, drunkenness, and violence; they were all inherited from Adam's fall from grace. This is called the sinful nature, and it is fused with man's eternal spirit. Man is naturally inclined toward these things.

In the garden of Eden, there were two trees. God told them not to touch the tree of knowledge of good and evil, or death would result. Man was given a soul to make the conscious choice. When the serpent crept into the garden, he appealed to Eve's flesh. He suggested something was lacking, and in eating the fruit, she would become wise and be like God. Eve apparently forgot she was already made in His perfect image; she was complete. Satan's suggestion manufactured an artificial void that would be fulfilled once she ate the forbidden fruit. The world system today uses the same concept in marketing and advertising, the power of suggestion to fabricate a need.

Once Adam and Eve disobeyed, they were forced to live by the tree of knowledge rather than the tree of life. The tree of knowledge has this insatiable quest for knowledge, but it never comes to the knowledge of the truth. What is the truth? The truth is: they traded spirit for flesh, life for death. Beware that Christians can have God's Spirit and still be led by the flesh. Eve was in the very presence of God and chose to believe Satan's false promise. Prayer and fasting can subdue the flesh, bringing it into submission to the Spirit. It starves the flesh man who is ever ready to come back to pursue the material world kingdom as the blessing of the Lord.

ANCHOR POINT

We are spiritually complete in God's salvation. While things may or may not be materially prosperous in this life, Satan uses the desire to keep our mind occupied with dreams of opulent success. In the end, it fades only to birth a new desire.

Kingdom of God
Evidence—The Fruit of the Spirit

> "But the fruit of the Spirit is love, joy, peace, longsuffering, kindness, goodness and faithfulness" (Galatians 5:22).

In my vision, the plain white box was empty. It then was filled with a brilliant light, and the words of the fruit of the Spirit were spoken. The fruit of the Spirit is the evidence for the kingdom of God. This is one of the most important issues for Christians to understand. You will know men by their fruit. That is spiritual fruit from a spiritual kingdom.

To produce fruit, you must abide in Christ. "I am the vine; you are the branches. He who abides in Me, and I in him, bears much fruit, for apart from Me, you can do nothing" (John 15:5). Without Christ, a Christian can be in danger of becoming a dried-out branch, looking for fig leaves to cover up. Simply adding Jesus to our busy life does not produce kingdom fruit. The evidence of growth is cultivated in the spiritual soil of prayer, fasting, repentance, study, fellowship, and worship.

James 1:2 says, "My brethren, count it all joy when you fall into various trials." It takes time to cultivate and grow fruit on a tree. The trials and tests are fertilizer for the fruit tree, making it strong and mature. Jesus walked past a fig tree and cursed it even though it was not the season for fruit. That tells us to be prepared in and out of season, not just when times are good.

The tree of knowledge sets seekers on an ambitious quest, producing fruit that glorifies the flesh. The tree of life produces the fruit of the Spirit. Jesus said, "Come to Me, all of you who labor and are heavy laden, and I will give you rest" (Matthew 11:28). Rest from seeking world ambitions and leave illusions behind. The fruit of the Spirit brings peace. This peace is from God and surpasses all understanding, which the world can never understand.

ANCHOR POINT

Being shaped by the influence of the Holy Spirit, those who walk in the spirit pattern their life after Jesus Christ. You will know them by their fruit.

Kingdom of Heaven
Evidence—Faith

> "Now faith is the substance of things hoped for, the evidence of things not seen" (Hebrews 11:1).

How is faith the evidence of the kingdom of heaven? Faith is unseen but is the material needed to build a kingdom foundation while here on earth. The world kingdom puts faith in building kingdoms that will perish. Putting trust in careers, wealth, homes, and relationships and using them as evidence of our faith is something God may test us with. Job and Abraham were examples of genuine faith. The material world is only temporary, and we are only pilgrims here. Without faith in the Lord Jesus, no one will enter through the gates of the future kingdom of heaven, as He is the way, the truth and the life. It really is all about Jesus.

Hebrews 13:14 says, "For here we have no continuing city, but we seek the one to come." The continuing city is "Thy Kingdom come," the future eternal city of the New Jerusalem. We cannot enter the continuing city without faith because it cannot be seen. Hebrews 11:6 tells us, "But without faith it is impossible to please Him." Even though God gave them everything, Adam and Eve lost the kingdom because they believed the serpent. Later, Abraham became the father of faith, because he believed God. From Abraham came the three faiths of the world: Judaism, Christianity, and Islam. All were seeded from Abraham as God said, "In your seed all the nations of the earth shall be blessed because you obeyed My voice" (Genesis 22:18). In His mercy, God sent His Son to return the kingdom, but faith is the substance needed to build our foundation, one experience at a time. And lastly, "By faith we understand the worlds were framed by the Word of God, so that the things which are seen were not made of things which are visible" (Hebrews 11:3).

ANCHOR POINT

Faith is believing God's character, believing He is who He says He is, believing His promises, even though we do not see them. By faith, we are building the foundation for the things we hope for, the continuing city, the New Jerusalem in the kingdom of heaven.

10. MINISTRY

The ministries of condemnation, reconciliation, and worship are all maintained within their respective kingdoms. The ministry is the service each kingdom offers distinctly. Each kingdom ministry has a main function to perform within its domain.

Kingdom of the World
Ministry—Condemnation

> "He who believes in Him is not condemned but he who does not believe is condemned already, because he has not believed in the name of the only begotten Son of God" (John 3:18).

The world kingdom was condemned at the fall of man. The word *condemn* means to pronounce guilty, sentence, or deem unfit for use. The ministry of condemnation rules the world, as every man born has a *condemned* nature because he has inherited sin and death. In the prison system, someone on death row is still walking around but condemned to die; the judgment has been given, and he or she is living until the appointed time. Also, a condemned building still stands but is unfit for use.

After meeting with God, Moses put a veil over his face until the glory of his countenance passed away. "For if the ministry of condemnation had glory, the ministry of righteousness exceeds much more in glory" (2 Corinthians 3:9). The world kingdom has its glory but only for a season. Before Adam trespassed, God's kingdom on earth had *eternal glory*. After the fall, death was introduced. "For the wages of sin is death" (Romans 6:23). Adam's then glorified body changed from eternal to perishable and unfit for living in the eternal kingdom of heaven.

Jesus was not sent to condemn the world. It was condemned at the fall. He came to fulfill the law and bring the new covenant into the world. "This is the judgement, that the light has come into the world, and men loved darkness rather than light" (John 3:19).

Leaving the ministry of condemnation and being reborn in the Holy Spirit, people enter into the new covenant and receive the ministry of reconciliation.

ANCHOR POINT

We are born into a fallen world with a sinful nature. This inheritance was passed down to us from Adam. Jesus came to set us free from condemnation and offer us the ministry of reconciliation.

Kingdom of God
Ministry—Reconciliation

> "Who has reconciled us to Himself through Jesus Christ and given us the ministry of reconciliation" (2 Corinthians 5:18).

The white box was empty because it represented the spiritual kingdom of God. You cannot see spirit. Jesus said His kingdom is not of this world, as this present world is temporal. The will of the Father was to reconcile us back to Him. *Reconcile* means to be in peace or to settle or resolve an issue. The issue is that man broke his covenant with God, resulting in death, and lost God's eternal kingdom on earth. Jesus is called the second Adam because only two men were born without a sinful nature: Adam and Jesus. All the sins of the world were poured onto Jesus at His crucifixion. The scripture says there is no forgiveness of sins without the shedding of blood. So, we plead the blood of Jesus, asking for forgiveness through the blood of the Lamb. When John saw Jesus, he said, "Look the Lamb of God!" (John 1:29). He is the Lamb of God for the sacrifice of the reconciliation. Once Jesus rose, the restoration was settled for all eternity. That is the reason there is no condemnation for those in Christ Jesus. The moment we believe in our hearts and receive His Holy Spirit, we pass from death to life, from condemnation to reconciliation. We will be found not guilty and counted among the righteous and members of His own family.

In return, we trade our old lives in, for the new life that He offers us through His sacrifice on the cross. My daily prayer is this: "Blessed are you, Father, King of the universe, who has fulfilled all the law through Jesus Christ the Messiah, and He has covered us in His righteousness." Jesus is our sacrifice and Savior, and we are covered in His righteousness for the reconciliation between us and God.

ANCHOR POINT

In the ministry of reconciliation, there is a wonderful joy ahead for us, even though the going can be rough for a while down here.

Kingdom of Heaven
Ministry—Worship

> "After these things I heard a loud voice of a great multitude in heaven, saying Alleluia! Salvation and glory and honor and power belong to the Lord our God!" (Revelation 19:1).

Heaven is a place of worship. The kingdom of heaven is the destination of the redeemed who endure until the end. The kingdom of heaven is both a spiritual and physical kingdom, and worship is the main ministry in heaven. Lucifer was the covering cherub in the throne of heaven. He was created with heavenly musical abilities to lead heaven's worship. He was God's most gifted angel, so he was given the highest service in heaven—worship. Lucifer malfunctioned on account of his beauty and great wealth, and pride filled him with the desire to rise above God. Then began a great war in heaven, where he led a rebellion against God and was thrown out. As a result, Satan uses the power of charisma and music in the world kingdom to keep people under his influence. Satan operates through the flesh of people's eye and ear gates. When God created man, He was designed to worship someone or something greater than himself. When man does not worship God, he finds something else to fix his praise upon. When the worship goes outside of God, it becomes idol worship. Idol worship and self-worship are from the realm of Satan and were the first sin before man's fall.

The book of Revelation tells of future events of the mysteries of heaven. It is a picture of the kingdom of heaven. In my vision, I saw a gold box containing brilliant precious gems. Revelation shows great bursts of light flashed, as it described glittering diamonds, rubies, and emeralds encircling His throne. It goes on to describe the twenty-four elders with white clothes and golden crowns upon their heads, casting their crowns in worship of Him. They worship Him day after day and night after night, saying, "Holy, holy, holy, Lord God Almighty—Who was, and is, and is to come!" (Revelation 4:8).

ANCHOR POINT

God's presence lives in the worship of those who worship Him in spirit and in truth. Learn to worship Him now because heaven is all about the ministry of worship.

11. TABERNACLE/TEMPLE

The Tabernacle was a moveable sanctuary made with a specific design to house the Ark of the Covenant. The Temple was the permanent home of the Tabernacle, using the same pattern God directed Moses to use on Mt. Sinai. It has three main sections: the Outer Court, the Holy Place, and the Most Holy Place.

Kingdom of the World
Temple—Outer Court

> "Then you shall set the altar of the burnt offering before
> the door of the tabernacle of the tent of meeting. And you
> shall set the laver between the tabernacle of meeting and
> put water in it" (Exodus 40:6–7).

The kingdom of the world is characterized by the Outer Court in the temple. The Outer Court represents the world in need of salvation, in need of an acceptable sacrifice for the sinful nature we are born with. The Outer Court had two objects: the bronze laver, which was used by the priests to wash and purify before entering the Temple, and the bronze altar, the place for sacrifice to atone for the sins of the people. If Adam had not sinned, there would be no need for sacrifice, for without the shedding of blood, there is no forgiveness of sins. Significantly before entering God's presence, one must be cleansed.

Interestingly, the entrance to the tabernacle or temple was called the wide gate. It was the gate where the people would come to bring offerings and animal sacrifices. All people were allowed in the Outer Court; it was the only area of the temple where non-Jews were allowed. The person bringing the sacrifice would place his or her hand on the head of the animal during the killing. It signified the animal took the person's place. The bronze laver was for the washing of our sins with the blood of the Lamb, Jesus. The bronze altar was at the cross, the place of sacrifice. The Lamb of God was sacrificed outside the gates of the city.

God is pouring out His Spirit to all people in the outer court of the world. But if people do not repent by washing in the blood of Jesus (the bronze laver) and then go to the bronze altar to claim His sacrifice, they will remain unchanged and unable to receive the outpouring of the Spirit. They remain in the Outer Court. Acts 2:38 said, "Repent and let everyone of you be baptized in the name of Jesus Christ for the remission of your sins and you shall receive the gift of the Holy Spirit." If you are standing in the Outer Court, wash, asking for the forgiveness of your sins and allowing Jesus to become your Lord and Savior. Keep praying and seeking until you receive His Holy Spirit. Then enter His presence in the Holy Place.

God said in the last days He would pour out His Spirit on all flesh (Acts 2:17). The Outer Court of the Tabernacle is symbolic of the world and those in need of salvation into His Holy Place. Even though Christians have accepted Jesus, there is still a need to be cleansed from the world as long as we are here.

Kingdom of God
Temple—The Holy Place

> "But you are a chosen race, a royal priesthood, a holy nation,
> a people for His possession" (1 Peter 2:9).

The empty white box represents the spiritual kingdom of God. No one can enter unless he is reborn in the Holy Spirit. Before we are reborn, we are standing in the Outer Court of the Tabernacle.

Only the Levite priests were permitted to enter the Holy Place. Their job was to be a mediator between the people and God. Inside the Holy Place, the priests oversaw the golden lampstand, the table of showbread, and the altar of incense. The Temple items point to Jesus as the light in the world (lampstand), the royal priesthood is the prayers of the saints (incense), and the bread (showbread) represents Jesus as the bread of life.

The Temple veil hung between the Holy Place and the Most Holy Place. The veil of separation was torn at His death. Jesus's torn body is now the entrance into the new covenant between man and God. The new covenant is eternal just like the kingdom we will live in, which is why the order of the Melchizedek priesthood is forever, with Jesus as our High Priest. The Levite high priest, unlike Jesus, had to be replaced at death. A new high priest then had to be appointed. We are now priests for the kingdom of God. As intercessors, we stand in the gap for those in need of prayer and those who are standing in the outer court. We carry the Tabernacle wherever we go. The people of the church are now the people of the covenant.

ANCHOR POINT

In the Tabernacle / Temple, only priests could enter the Holy Place. It was part of the priest's ministry to keep the lamp burning perpetually. Today, members of God's holy family intercede for others, keeping our light shining continually.

Kingdom of Heaven
Temple—The Most Holy Place / Holy of Holies

> "For a tabernacle was prepared: the first part, in which was
> the lampstand and the table, and the showbread which
> is called the sanctuary. And behind the second veil, the
> part of the tabernacle which is called the Holiest of All"
> (Hebrews 9:2–3).

The kingdom of heaven is the home of God, the Most Holy Place. It is also called the Holy of Holies and the Inner Room. The Most Holy Place was the presence of God on earth. It was the centerpiece for the nation of Israel. God instructed Moses to build an ark to house the Tablets of the Law, the covenant He wrote for them. God revealed to Moses the precise pattern and design of the Tabernacle. The Most Holy Place's dimensions were the same height and length, forming a perfect square, covered with pure gold. The same dimensions were given for the New Jerusalem, a square box too. The Most Holy Place was made as a copy of the sanctuary in heaven. The veil between the Holy Place and the Most Holy Place represented the separation between God and man. The only object in the Inner Room was the golden Ark of the Covenant. Only the high priest was allowed in and only one time per year to heal the sins of the nation. It is called Yom Kippur, the Day of Atonement. The high priest came in with blood and a rope tied to his waist in case his offering was not accepted. The high priest had tingling bells on his robe, and if the bells went silent, they pulled him out before he would die. The contents inside the Ark of the Covenant were the Tablets of the Law, Aaron's rod, and the jar with manna.

The high priest was required to sprinkle blood on the mercy seat (the top cover of the ark). The mercy seat was the most sacred place, as it is the ultimate place of appeal for God's grace. After Jesus resurrected, He entered heaven and presented Himself to the Father. He paid the price for us. Becoming our High Priest, in the order of Melchizedek, He then sprinkled His own blood on the mercy seat for our eternal debt. We now have a new covenant because of His sacrifice. The law is now fulfilled. No more sacrifice is ever needed. He has deposited His Holy Spirit in us as a guarantee of the promise we will be with Him in His Most Holy Place, the kingdom of heaven, forever.

ANCHOR POINT

The veil between Holy Place and the Most Holy Place was torn at Jesus's death, ending the separation between God and man. We can now come boldly to the throne of grace. We now represent Him in the earth, as our bodies are the temples that house His Holy Spirit.

12. THE THREE FEASTS

When Israel was living in the kingdom of Judah, they were commanded to observe three pilgrimage festivals annually. "Three times in the year, all your men shall appear before the Lord, the Lord God of Israel" (Exodus 34:23): the Passover (Pesach), Pentecost (Shavuot), and Tabernacles (Sukkot).

The Kingdom of the World
Three Feasts—Passover

> "The next day John saw Jesus coming toward him and said, 'Behold the Lamb of God who takes away the sin of the world!'" (John 1:29).

The Passover is represented by the kingdom of the world, because if Adam had never sinned, the Passover would never have been instituted. Jesus would have no reason to come down to redeem man from sin and death. The Passover was the feast in remembrance of how the angel of death "passed over" the Israelites' homes. God intentionally hardened Pharaoh's heart with each of the ten plagues. He wanted to make a distinction between His chosen nation and Egypt, using death as the dividing factor. He wanted Israel to be certain it was He who delivered them. Moses was instructed to tell Israel to take a lamb, sacrifice it, and apply the blood over the doorposts. When the angel of death came, he passed over the houses with the blood and struck all the Egyptian houses. It was after the Exodus that God brought them to Mt. Sinai and gave them their laws and Tabernacle instructions as they agreed to His Holy covenant for their nation. They had two other feasts that were incorporated into Passover: The Feast of Unleavened Bread and the Feast of First Fruits. They are all celebrated during the Passover season. John the Baptist first identifies Jesus as the Lamb of God. Jesus's mission was to come down from heaven and give His life so we can pass over death. Therefore, He was crucified on Passover to bring us the new covenant for eternal life. His one-time death fulfilled the requirement of all the daily animal sacrifices from the old covenant laws. Jesus's body represents the unleavened bread with the stripes. He said, "Take, eat; this is my body ... for this is My Blood of the new covenant" (Matthew 26:26–28). Just like God commanded Israel to commemorate the Passover, Jesus commands us to remember His suffering and sacrifice. Jesus rose on the third day of the Passover, the day of the First Fruits.

"But in fact, Christ has been raised from the dead, the first fruits of those who have fallen asleep" (1 Corinthians 15:20). The scripture continues with "For since by man came death, by Man also came the resurrection of the dead" (1 Corinthians 15:21). Jesus, who was sacrificed on Passover, marks the beginning of the new covenant to deliver all people from death.

ANCHOR POINT

Jesus came willingly as the Lamb of God to "pass us over" from death to life. He commands us to remember His sacrifice, which brings the new covenant between man and God until He returns.

Kingdom of God
Three Feasts—Pentecost

> "And it will shall come to pass in the last days, says God,
> That I will pour out of My Spirit on all flesh" (Acts 2:17).

The Pentecost marks the advent of the Holy Spirit and fulfillment of the new covenant for all. He states in Joel 2:28 (Old Testament) and Acts 2:17 (New Testament), "I will pour out my Spirit on all people." Shavuot is the giving of the law to His chosen nation, Israel, and Pentecost commemorates the giving of the Holy Spirit. Pentecost is also known as Shavuot and the Feast of Weeks.

After the Passover in Egypt, Israel fled into the wilderness. It was on the fiftieth day from the first Passover that the law was given on Mt. Sinai. In the Greek language, the word for fifty is *Pentecost*. At the giving of the Law, the covenant between God and Israel, they agreed to obey and be His people and sealed the covenant with the sprinkling of blood. God's covenant is His highest honor. He had the Tabernacle built just to house the Ark of the Covenant. His mercy seat dwells on the cover. It was separated with a veil, and only the high priest could enter in and only one time per year with blood to sprinkle on the mercy seat. His covenant shows we belong to Him!

Before Jesus died, He told His disciples to go to Jerusalem and wait. On the day of Pentecost, fifty days after the death of Jesus, His disciples were gathered in the upper room when a rushing wind from heaven filled the whole house. Tongues of fire rested upon their heads, and they were all filled with the Holy Spirit. Pentecost and the receiving of the Holy Spirit belong to the kingdom of God because we need to receive His Holy Spirit to enter His kingdom while still here on earth.

ANCHOR POINT

Pentecost is the giving of the law in the Old Testament and the Spirit in the New Testament. Being reborn in His Spirit, we can enter the kingdom of God and finally the kingdom of Heaven.

Kingdom of Heaven
Three Feasts—Tabernacles

> "Now we know that if the earthly tent we live in is destroyed,
> we have a building from God, an eternal house in heaven"
> (2 Corinthians 5:1).

The kingdom of heaven is God's promise to man. The Feast of Tabernacles is the reminder of His faithfulness while Israel journeyed for forty years in the wilderness. This feast is connected to the kingdom of heaven because it represents the ingathering of the harvest. The Passover is the planting season, Pentecost is the grain harvest, and Tabernacles is the ingathering at the year's end. While here, we are to bear fruit. The goal is to produce a harvest, as Christ uses His people to bring God's salvation to a broken, fallen world. During the wilderness journey, the Israelites stayed in temporary tent shelters. Sukkot is the feast marking God's provisions and care for them. During the celebration of Tabernacles, or Sukkot, there were three things they were required to do to remember God's faithfulness.

1. Cover the booths with special plants
2. Live in the Booths for seven days
3. Rejoice before the Lord

Rejoicing before the Lord at the Feast of Tabernacles was to show gratitude for God's protection and provision, as He kept them safely before the Promised Land. Jesus says, "Do not rejoice in this, that the spirits are subject unto you, but rather rejoice because your names are written in heaven" (Luke 10:20). We rejoice today because we have faith in God's promises and provision because He said so and we believe Him. We are to live in the world as pilgrims passing through, in our earthly tents preparing for our heavenly home. "For our citizenship is in heaven, from which we also eagerly wait for the Savior, the Lord Jesus Christ, who will transform our lowly body that it may be conformed to His glorious body" (Philippians 3:20). The Feast of Tabernacles represents the final harvest when all people whose names are written in the Lamb's book of life will share in the joy and blessings of the kingdom of heaven forever. "Praise Him with the sound of the trumpet. Praise Him with the lute and harp! Praise Him with the timbrel and dance. Praise Him with the stringed instruments and flutes. Praise Him with loud cymbals; Praise Him with clashing cymbals! Let everything that has breath, Praise the Lord!" Psalm 150:3–6.

ANCHOR POINT

On our journey, rejoice because God is faithful in His promise and provision, reminding us of our status as pilgrims since our true home is in the eternal kingdom of heaven.

13. THE END GAME

The kingdoms have been explored and illustrated for a better understanding. The end game is determined by the life we choose while here on earth. Each kingdom has an end game with a unique destination that fulfills its ultimate purpose as it relates to the kingdoms and the three boxes.

The Kingdom of the World
The End Game—Hell

> "I am He who lives, and as dead, and behold I am alive forevermore. Amen. And I have the keys of hell and death" (Revelation 1:18).

People talk about salvation, declaring, "I'm saved." My question used to be "Saved from what?" Salvation is to be free from the sinful nature. The sin nature cannot live in the presence of God. This is why we plead the blood of Jesus. Before disobeying God's Word, Adam was warned he would die. Since then, death has passed to every living being on earth. For that reason, we get sick, become old, and naturally die. God in His divine mercy sent Jesus to free us, giving man the choice to reconcile to the Father. Most people are not aware that unless they are redeemed, they are automatically destined for eternal separation from God, which is hell. After death, we do not get a second chance. Man, in his current state, cannot enter heaven with his sinful nature. Some may think confessing His name, attending church activities, and making tithes and offerings clear them of hell's fire. No, there must be a circumcision of the heart, progression of sanctification, examination, and praying with humble repentance. You must transfer from the kingdom of darkness to the kingdom of light before passing, or it will be too late.

The Kingdom of the World
The End Game—Hell

Born Once, Die Twice

The scripture states, "And it is appointed for men to die once but after this the judgement" (Hebrews 9:27). What does it mean to be born once and die twice? Being born and dying in the flesh is one birth and one death. The person who retains his or her sinful nature at death stays locked in the world kingdom box. Imagine the bottom floor of the box dropping out at death and the person tumbling into darkness and landing in a holding place. That place is Hades or hell. What is the second death? Revelation 20:14 says, "Then Death and Hades were thrown into the lake of fire. This is the second death. And anyone not found written in the Book of Life, was cast into the lake of fire." Hades acts as the temporary jail for the unsaved, until judgment day. The second death will come after the sounding of the seventh trumpet, when Christ returns, and judgment on all people and things. The second death is the spirit's eternal death in the lake of fire. God's hope is for all to transfer into His kingdom before the first death. Jesus says in Revelation 1:18, "And I have the keys of Hades and of Death." This placement is final and a permanent destination. In choosing Christ, there is no Hades or second death. "That I have set before you life and death, blessing and cursing; therefore, choose life, that both you and your descendants may live" (Deuteronomy 30:19). Today, choose life.

·ANCHOR POINT

Jesus compels us not to die in our sins (John 8:24). It is a fixed state and cannot be negotiated after death. Hell is described as a place of torment and the opposite of paradise, where there is peace and rest. Hell is the end of all games (2 Thessalonians 1:9).

Kingdom of God
The End Game—Paradise

> "Then he said to Jesus, 'Lord remember me when You come into Your Kingdom.' And Jesus said to him, 'Assuredly, I say to you, today you will be with Me in Paradise'" (Luke 23:42).

The tomb was empty, as Jesus had risen from the dead. The white box was empty too! It represents the spiritual kingdom of God that man must enter before his death. Jesus said, "My Kingdom is not of this world" (John 18:36), meaning it is in the spiritual heavenly realm. We must accept Him now, be reborn in His Holy Spirit, before we leave our flesh behind.

Born Twice, Die Once

The meaning of "born twice, die once" is the first birth is flesh, and the second birth is the spiritual birth in the Holy Spirit. But physical death is once. At rebirth, eternal life begins. That is why Jesus told Nicodemus, "Unless one is born again, he cannot see the Kingdom of God" (John 3:3). When someone transfers from the kingdom of darkness to the kingdom of light, I imagine the red world box unfolds its six-paneled walls into a simple white cross. It sets us free from perishing into an eternal second death.

The story of the rich man and the beggar tells of spiritual destinations after death. "So it was the beggar died, and was carried by the angels into Abraham's bosom. And being in torments in Hades, he lifted up his eyes and saw Abraham from afar, and Lazarus in his bosom" (Luke 16:23). The rich man had no compassion while living; he made fun of the poor. After dying, he looked across and saw the poor man in Abraham's abode. He asked him to come dip his finger in water to cool his tongue. Abraham told him it was not possible because there was a big chasm that no one could cross. Abraham's abode, or the bosom of Abraham, is paradise. Jesus told the thief on the cross, "Today you will be with me in Paradise" (Luke 23:42), because he believed Jesus at His death. Paradise is the resting place of the righteous until the great day of judgment.

We will all stand before the throne of the Lord, and those whose names are written in the Lamb's book He will declare "not guilty," and then He will say, "Enter into the gates," where there will be joy, peace, and no more suffering or death for eternity.

ANCHOR POINT

God has prepared a place for those who have washed their robes in the blood of the Lamb. You must be born again to enter His rest. Paradise is the resting place of the righteous until the final judgement. There is rest in paradise (RIP).

The Kingdom of Heaven
The End Game—The New Jerusalem

> "In My Father's house are many mansions; if it were not so, I would have told you; I go to prepare a place for you" (John 14:2).

The gold box represents the New Jerusalem, Zion, the eternal city of the kingdom of heaven. Revelation tells of its glory by describing the foundations as adorned with every kind of precious stone. In my vision, there were brilliant gems covering the inside of the golden box. Coming down out of heaven, the Holy City is described as prepared like a bride adorned for her husband. It says, "Let us be glad and rejoice and give Him glory, for the marriage of the Lamb has come, and His wife, has made herself ready" (Revelation 19:7).

The book of Revelation is the vision of the future kingdom of heaven. It is the end game of all end games. It begins with the Lamb opening the scroll and the breaking of the seven seals, the seals on man and in the earth from Adam's original sin. After the seventh trumpet sounds, the angel calls out, "The kingdoms of this world have become the kingdoms of our Lord and of His Christ and He shall reign forever and ever!" (Revelation 11:15). The kingdoms are all now one, with one ruler: God, the Father, the Son, and the Holy Spirt.

The great judgment is called. "Death and Hades were cast into the lake of fire. This is the second death. And anyone not found written in the Book of Life was cast into the lake of fire" (Revelation 20:14). After judgment, the curse is gone. In the kingdom of heaven, nothing evil will ever enter. He will wipe away every tear from our eyes and suffering and death will no longer exist because the previous things have all passed away (Revelation 21:1). The victor will inherit all these things; He will be their God, and they will be His people returning to what Adam lost, eternal life with God. The words of the Lord's Prayer are finally fulfilled: "Your Kingdom come, Your Will be done, on earth as it is in heaven" (Matthew 6:10).

In the end, the tree of life, guarded after Adam's fall, returns in the New Jerusalem, allowing us access to eat from it again. We can come and receive the reward He has prepared, where we will live with Him in the kingdom of heaven forever. Amen.

Those who have received Jesus as Lord and Savior are laborers with Christ and celebrate with Him at the wedding in the New Jerusalem. The new covenant is confirmed and sealed with the blood of the Lamb. Blessed are those who are invited to the wedding feast of the Lamb. Hallelujah! (Revelation 19:9).

FINAL THOUGHTS

Although this world is not my home, but your
kingdom here is worth fighting for ...
—Brian Courtney Wilson, "Worth Fighting For"

The Bible is a divine work dictated by God and therefore has multiple levels and intricate layers of meaning. We should always study to show ourselves approved by spending time exploring the deeper meanings and revelation of God's Holy Word. *The Three Boxes: Book of Kingdoms* is simply a modern vision to illustrate the characteristics of the differences between the kingdom of the world, the kingdom of God, and the kingdom of heaven. I invite you to study the meaning behind the three boxes to gain a vision of God's kingdom, as He has revealed them for this purpose. If you have never invited Jesus into your life as your Savior, please ask Him. He loves you dearly. The ultimate destination is the kingdom of heaven, exemplified with the golden box and precious gems. The biggest takeaway of the kingdoms journey is that we must be born again to enter the kingdom of God, and it must be entered in this lifetime. The Bible clearly states that man was created in His image (Genesis 1:27), and we will be alive somewhere, forever—either in the presence of God, enjoying glorious fellowship, or separated in the torments of hell. There are only two possibilities. In my vision, after all the boxes were presented, I asked the Spirit, "What did this all mean?"

The Spirit said, "To seek first the kingdom of God and His righteousness and all these things shall be added to you" (Matthew 6:33).

In 2012, when I first saw the vision, I was thinking inside the box. Today, I realize that the things He referred to are not necessarily in the red box but in the kingdom of heaven, the New Jerusalem, where the covenant is confirmed, and man will once again have eternal life with Him. God bless you. My prayer is that through His Word, He will show you the true purpose of life here in this kingdom and the one to come. Amen.

With gladness,
Elaine Faucett